Make Your Own Finger Puppets!

Tips & Techniques for Fabulous Fun

Puppets designed by

Raffaella Dowling

Photography by F. William Lagaret

Text by Alan Carr

Mud Puddle inc.
NEW YORK

P9-CPX-554

Make Your Own Finger Puppets!
Tips & Techniques for Fabulous Fun

Puppets designed by Raffaella Dowling
Photography by F. William Lagaret
Text by Alan Carr

Published by
Mud Puddle, Inc.
36 W. 25th Street
New York, NY 10010
info@mudpuddleinc.com

ISBN: 978-1-60311-206-2

Printed in China

Contents

INTRODUCTION

Puppets, which have a rich history in cultures all across the globe, come in every form imaginable. Finger puppets, with their small size and adorable details, have an extra special charm. And, best of all, they are easy to create using inexpensive materials found at your local craft store or around your own house!

Making finger puppets is a wonderful way to learn craft techniques and explore creative ideas. You can build animals, people, mythical beings, or anything else you can imagine! Developing these enchanting characters can be a great way of entertaining yourself, but you can also expand the fun by inviting other aspiring puppeteers to join in.

For example, invite several friends to share the dismantled fingers from an old glove along with some craft materials. Have a contest to see who can come up with the most imaginative puppet (based on everyone having the same stuff to work with). You'll be amazed at how unique and individual the solutions are!

Once you've made your finger puppets, it's rewarding and fun to entertain the people around you with puppet shows. And, puppets make wonderful gifts, especially if you design them with the recipient in mind. Give grandma a puppet of her favorite animal or your best friend a puppet of their favorite movie character.

Finger puppets are compact enough that you can always bring one along wherever you go. They're cute enough that everyone will want you to bring them one too!

Basic Tools and Materials:

The cut-off fingers of a glove: Anything that sits securely and comfortably on your finger can be the foundation of your puppet. But extracting the fingers from a glove is often the easiest solution. Gloves that are no longer being used, or who have lost their mates, or pairs purchased at a dollar store, can be easily recycled into an array of exciting new characters. Best of all, each glove has five "fingers" which will give you multiple chances to experiment and perfect a your puppet. Or, if you choose, you can use one glove to create a whole puppet family!

DESIGN TIP

When you are creating your finger puppet, take inspiration from the type of glove you are using! For example, the finger from a yellow dish-washing glove might lead you to develop a rubber-ducky character, or a fisherman in a yellow rain-slicker. Patterned gloves are yet another fantastic starting point. Remember, interesting gloves make for interesting puppets!

Craft Glue is used to adhere materials and objects to your finger puppet. Craft glue provides a strong bond and, if it gets on your hands (or anything else), it's easy to clean up with soap and water.

Scissors are the safest and most effective way to cut materials like felt, pipe cleaners or thread. Always be careful using scissors, and have an adult help.

Fabric paint or permanent markers are useful for drawing and coloring in features and details on your puppet character. - - - ┐

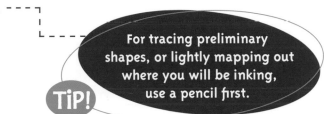

TiP! For tracing preliminary shapes, or lightly mapping out where you will be inking, use a pencil first.

Felt is a sturdy, inexpensive craft cloth that comes in a variety of colors. With scissors, glue and a little imagination, felt can be used to build clothing, wings and props for your puppet pals. The easiest way to use felt is to cut out flat shapes and either glue them onto your sock structure, or layer them together for interesting effects.

Great props don't have to be complicated. Create easy bananas with just some simple yellow & green felt shapes, and you'll have a very funky monkey!

Make your puppet King of the Jungle by constructing its lion's mane and tail from yellow and brown felt. Arranging the **mane** on the front of the puppet, and the **tail** on the back, achieves a nice sense of depth. Roar!!

Felt can also be cut and glued in certain ways to create a 3-dimensional object or shape.

Create the shell of a snail from this flat pattern,

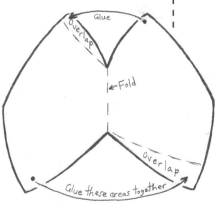

Glue

Overlap

←Fold

Overlap

Glue these areas together

and then mold it and glue it into a shape that is surprisingly round.

Cotton balls and small pom poms are perfect for creating individual features, like noses and ears, but can be bunched together as well, for a more textured look.

Glue a large, white cotton ball onto a white puppet, then embellish for a clever and cute polar bear head!

Cluster several small, **black pom-poms** densely together to make an impressive body for this creepy crawler!

Colored feathers are found in most craft stores and are ideal for adding texture, form and flamboyant flair to any puppet pal.

Make a parrot with personality, using multi-colored feathers of different sizes.

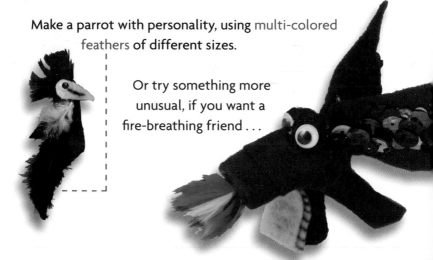

Or try something more unusual, if you want a fire-breathing friend . . .

Pipe Cleaners are perfect for creating slender arms, legs or other appendages. These lengths of "furry wire" are easy to cut, bend and shape into accessories, geometric shapes and coils.

Make slender legs for a flamingo, or furry legs for a spider.

Cut & twist pipe cleaners to make antennae for a bee or ladybug.

Colored thread is terrific for making hair, whiskers for your favorite animal, or creating other types of linear effects. Thread is also great for attaching things onto your puppet, but always ask an adult for help when sewing.

Googly eyes come in a variety of sizes and styles and instantly give life and personality to your puppet. They are inexpensive and available at most craft stores.

They can also be layered together with buttons, pom poms or sequins for a variety of interesting effects.

Buttons are great for making eyes, noses and other features and embellishments. They also make wonderful decorative elements on surfaces such as Ladybug wings.

Sequins are a great way to add some sparkle to your projects. Glue them onto your puppet to create a decorative or patterned effect such as this snazzy starfish!

Ribbon can be used to make certain kinds of hair or fur in addition to wonderful accessories such as clothing and belts.

Add a button, sequin or, in this case, a plastic rhinestone to your ribbon, and you have a poodle that is totally glam!

GALLERY
OF
FUN IDEAS

Insect Pals

Dragonfly

Ladybug

Snail

Butterfly

Bumble Bee

TiP!

Draw a "web" pattern with black marker on a white piece of felt to create a perfect home for this spider!

Spider

WiLd kingdom

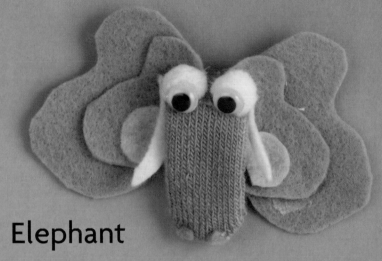

Elephant

TiP!

The "finger" part of the puppet doesn't necessarily have to be the "body" of your character. It can be a facial feature, like the trunk of this expressive elephant!

Polar Bear

Zebra

Lion

Snake

Monkey

Panda

TiP!

Try using felt to create background elements to your puppet. Cut a tree-shape out of a piece of green felt, and your giraffe will have some tall foliage to munch on!

Giraffe

Bunny

Skunk

Woodland Critters

Owl

Eagle

Masters
of the
House

Cat

TiP!

Think about fun accessories that your puppet character would enjoy. With a little glue and creativity, you can give your cat a colorful ball of yarn to play with!

Poodle

Dog

Farmyard
Fun

Cow

Pig

TiP!

White pom poms, when glued closely together, can make a wonderful wool coat for your fluffy sheep.

Sheep

Turkey

Under the Sea

Sea

Seahorse

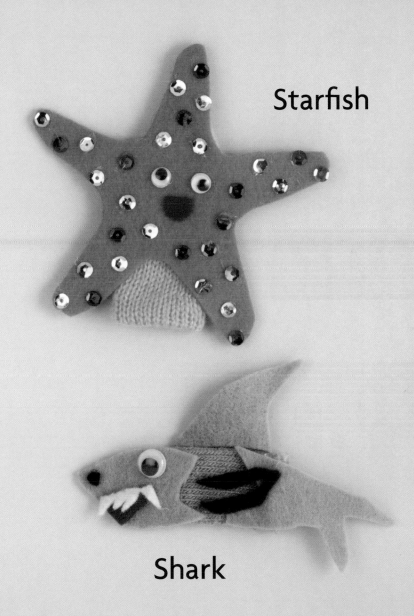

Starfish

Shark

Sea Turtle

Clownfish

TiP!

Think of unusual ways
to use items like googly eyes.
This octopus is ready to give you
a hug with his tentacles and
"eye-catching" suction cups!

Octopus

Feathered

Canary

Friends

Parrot

Penguin

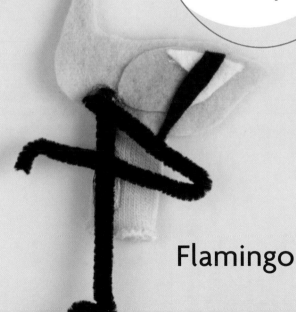

TiP!

Sometimes felt shapes need a bit of underlying support. Glue small lengths of wood dowel behind the neck & body of this flamingo, to help the puppet keep its shape.

Flamingo